Eva is a chosen daughter, wife, mother, grandmother, teacher, principal, principal coach and educational consultant. She has devoted her adult life to pursuing her vision of supporting students through her work in public education. At the age of seven, Eva knew she wanted to follow her mother's example and become a teacher. After graduating from Southern Illinois University in Carbondale, Illinois, she began her teaching career and has enjoyed more than two decades as a classroom teacher and 19 years as an elementary school principal.

Under her leadership, the school has been recognized as an 'A School', 'High Performing School' and 'High Progress School'. She has received national and local recognition for her school leadership. Teaching has been her life's mission. When she became a principal, every day she saw herself as a teacher and used much of what she learned as a classroom teacher in her role as a principal. At the age of seven, the vision of becoming a teacher ignited a passion within her that has inspired her through every stage of her career and continues to live and motivate her today. This book is birthed out of her personal experience with the work of vision.

This book is dedicated to those whose love and support I have been blessed and privileged to receive:

My husband of 33 years and my best friend Dr. Eugene Earl Stevens, our children Charles, Erica, Elliott and Earl/Rhoda, and our grandchildren Madyssen, Mason, Etonde and Neema for the lasting bond of family.

My mother Quinetta Gillespie Harris, for her love, model and unceasing guidance.

My siblings, Tommy, J. Harris, Lorenzo Harris and Faye Harris for childhood experiences that created cherishable memories.

Eva Harris Stevens

VISION: A PILLAR OF LEADERSHIP

Simply Stated: A Resource for Understanding and Operating in Vision

AUSTIN MACAULEY PUBLISHERS™

LONDON • CAMBRIDGE • NEW YORK • SHARJAH

A CIP catalogue record for this title is available from the British Library.

ISBN 9781398403420 (Paperback)
ISBN 9781398416772 (Hardback)
ISBN 9781398403437 (ePub e-book)
ISBN 9781398417281 (Audiobook)

www.austinmacauley.com

First Published 2023
Austin Macauley Publishers Ltd®
1 Canada Square
Canary Wharf
London
E14 5AA

Honor to God for inspiring vision, for allowing me to operate in a continual union with vision through serving as an educator and though the writing of this book.

To those whose path of destiny intersected mine exemplified love and created lasting impressions.

- Eddie Jackson, who provided nurturing and support as my first principal.
- Jack Kensler who later hired me as a teacher and then as an assistant principal.
- Supervisors and colleagues for the seeds of professional efficacy.
- Every staff member who worked with me during my 19 years as a principal for their unique contributions to the team.
- Students whose presence, eyes, smiles and hugs caused me to dream bigger and work harder.
- To my circle of sisters for the gift of friendship.
- Dr. Warren H. Stewart, Sr. for his Biblical teachings and strong model of visionary leadership that helped to shape my life and work.

Table of Contents

Introduction

Early memories of school created in a small southern school in north central Mississippi, clearly defined the fundamental purpose of the school and revealed the inclusive and solid practices that inspired students to learn. The environment on these grounds and within these walls waved the invisible welcome banner evident in the voices and in the interactions. The language and sounds of high expectations filled the school community. These experiences created the picture of a healthy school and inflamed a vision for the work.

This book points out the critical need for clarity of vision. It illustrates the powerful and essential relationship between the leader and vision and how that connection kindles vision and leadership in others.

Simply Stated

A Resource for Understanding and Operating in Vision.

Section One

Clarity

The Charge of Vision

Clarity creates an impelling force that hastens forward.

From the beginning to the ultimate state, vision provides a firm and crucial support on which leadership unfolds. Many books, articles, tapes, lectures and sessions have focused on the importance of vision, but how many readers truly realize what it means? How many of us understand the deep significance of vision and are committed to embracing it in our life and work?

Vision is the ability to truly see with the eyes of the heart. The dream in the heart creates the image and reflects it on the backdrop of the mind, which captures the image and transfers it to the physical realm. Vision invites clarity, inspires a deep level of commitment and provokes high expectations that repel everything out of alignment with the oneness of what the heart, the mind and the eyes embrace. Seeing invites focus, determination, pushing and calling out. If there was a magic bullet to breed high expectations, it would be vision. Vision inspires one to look and see, to question and bring others into the realm of seeing.

The words, "Where there is no vision, the people perish." –Proverbs 29:18, may sit somewhere in the recesses of your mind. You may have heard them but discounted their meaning and significance. Vision points the feet and keeps them moving in a defined direction. It lifts the hands and causes them to hold up the picture. It clears the mind and allows it to focus. Vision creates a steady unquenchable passion that gently draws, wisely informs and carefully guides. Vision arms you with power when you personalize it and claim it for yourself.

Some of my earliest and fondest memories of being in classrooms and around the school with my mother, a teacher for more than thirty years, revealed my purpose and shaped my vision. Before reaching school age, I saw the school as an environment filled with learning, laughter, connections, high expectations, discipline and structure. Listening to the lessons and recitations by students, watching interactions, celebrations, writing on the chalk board, stacking the books, seeing my mother teach, engaging with fellow teachers and performing many other responsibilities captured my attention and shaped my thinking and play. The sounds and activities within the school pointed to purpose.

These early experiences created an impression within my heart that would later be echoed as, "I want to be a teacher, when I grow up."

The vision birthed in my heart at an early age became a reality when I graduated from college at 21 and began the career of my dreams as a third-grade teacher in an inner-city school. After more than two decades of embracing a vision for teaching, being guided by a passion for student learning and enjoying a career that filled my life with joy, I experienced an epiphany. The beckoning target that had faithfully guided my deep and unwavering passion for teaching was beginning to shift. This shifting ushered in an invitation to change, which was met with an emphatic 'NO.' Vision revealed its power to exercise dominion over no and anything outside of its trajectory and brought my thoughts to rest at the point of openness. Being open to receiving a new direction allowed me to perceive that this shifting was not a change in purpose, rather an enlargement of the vision. Understanding and accepting this shift enabled me to see myself as a school principal. New eyes helped me see the principal as simply an extension of the teacher with a broader sphere of influence capable of impacting the lives of more students. The principal is capable of ensuring that the entire school community is a warm, inviting, safe and learning-focused place where students are valued, want to be and where families feel good when they leave their children. Had this vision not shifted from teaching in the classroom to teaching from the role of principal, I would have happily spent an entire career as a classroom teacher.

In the fall of 2000, after serving four years as an assistant principal, I began my tenure as an elementary principal that covered a span of 19 years and proved to be among the most enjoyable and fulfilling times of my life. Every day of these 19 years required me to connect, reconnect and stay connected to my vision. The work required me to know the vision, be clear about what it meant to me and what I wanted for those I was connected to in this work.

It was a K-6 school with about 1200 students and more than 100 staff members. Many of the practices revealed the staff's concern for students and engaged them in fun activities. Overall proficiency levels were low. There were classrooms of second grade students who were unable to read. Largely the culture was adult centered, social and resistive to change. Parent involvement was non-existent. The school district was in the second year of implementing the district's strategic plan. Each school site was expected to develop and implement its plan aligned to the district's strategic plan. The school staff had not begun this work.

Vision spoke; it revealed that this school would impact the learning and the lives of students. Staff members would understand and accept their purpose and be clear about what they wanted for their students. The mission and vision would take root in the hearts of each staff member and live among us. The first year we worked collaboratively to identify our mission and vision.

Simultaneously, I conducted classroom observations and provided immediate feedback to create a climate of high expectations, accountability and trust while working to shape the vision for increasing students' learning outcomes.

In the second year we identified a professional development model that inspired teachers and began a process of empowerment that has continued through the years. The principal and teachers engaged in professional development specifically aligned to the needs of the school. We learned together, moved forward to implement this model with a sense of urgency and provided differentiated support for each teacher.

During my tenure, many teachers began as new teachers. The process of support and mentoring provided to these novice teachers resulted in them becoming highly effective teachers who transitioned to teacher leaders, assistant principals, principals, district office staff supporting schools, state education staff and international teachers. We celebrated the growth, development and advancement of these former novice teachers. Today, many of them support students and teachers in schools throughout the district, the state and the nation. The ongoing joyful shouts of celebrations for the highly effective teachers who transitioned out of the school, created instructional skills gaps each time vacancies were filled with new teachers. The strong professional development model and the foundation and structures on which the school culture had been shaped provided the framework and support needed to continually help the new and novice staff succeed in becoming highly effective teachers. This professional development model will be discussed in detail in section five.

Today, this school is a student-centered collaborative and focused school community that operates based on a common mission, vision, shared values, common goals and collective commitments. The adults understand that together they can ensure that all students develop their potential and fulfill their unique purpose. The adults in the school embrace their beckoning target that compels and motivates them to work together to create continual evidence of their effectiveness. The adults know how they must behave and the commitments they must make to one another as they work in teams and in school wide collaboration with others. The staff is committed to their own learning and the academic success of each student. Proactive leadership emulates from each staff member as they lead from their positions of influence. Teamwork is apparent as teachers and staff meet regularly to plan for student learning, reach out to seek support for themselves or assist others. Special area teachers and classified staff collaborate to support student learning. Parents are actively involved in the school, supporting their children at home and in taking advantage of opportunities provided by the school for their own growth and development.

We endured the revolt against classroom walkthroughs, transformed the lack of interest in professional development, stamped out the dislike for feedback, overturned the dismal student learning results, dispelled the bar of low expectations, pulled together the fractions of disbelief and plucked up the seeds of discard. The air is fresh. The scenery is beautiful. Little people and big people are happy. How did we get here? What road led us to this new place?

Guided by the light of the internal forecast, vision penetrates and launches beyond the sad eyes of fear and doubt to embrace the drum beat of new beginnings. The muscle of vision rescues us from the claws of darkness and sustains us by the internal flame of our commitment. Vision, recognizes and understands that the school is not about you, yet it is everything about you. It is about your ability to cast a wide net and understand that your sphere of positive and constructive influence is contingent upon your ability to operate from a position of clarity and sensitivity. A position that shows honor and unconditional respect for all, that treats others the way you want to be treated and the way you want them to treat others. Under the guidance of vision, the leader trains the staff, supports their growth and monitors and celebrates their effectiveness. Vision nurtures the greatness within the individuals and helps the team welcome second order changes that impact the organization. Vision reproduces vision that looks beyond the current reality and embraces the idea that there are no impossibilities.

Vision, recognizes and understands that the school is not about you, yet it is everything about you. It is about your ability to cast a wide net and understand that your sphere of positive and constructive influence is contingent upon your ability to operate from a position of clarity and sensitivity.

Section Two

Goals

The Direction of Vision

Goals identify the course along which the organization moves towards the vision.

Goals are the undeniable relationship between the current reality and what the organization can become. Recently, a colleague called to inform me that our English Learner reclassification rate was 41.7%. She shared that this percentage was 23% above the district average and possibly 20% above the state average. She went on to share that 41.7% was definitely an outlier. How would you celebrate 41.7% proficiency? Do you recognize that it is not your goal, but see it as a ten percent increase from the prior year and a step closer to the goal? Or do you see it as 23% above the district and 20% above the state results? Your commitment to what lies within your heart will force you to see your results only in competition with yourself. Without the eyes of vision, one is unable to see where they are going and tend to accept a lower level of performance.

Vision causes you to block out the insignificant and focus on what is paramount for you in the growth and achievement process.

Vision accounts for every student. It is aware of the current reality, but instead of focusing its attention on the conditions that are outside of its control, vision bars the door and conscientiously works to enhance and strengthen those factors over which it has dominance. In our school community, more than ninety percent of our students were on free and reduced lunches, indicating low socio-economic household income. Ninety percent of our students were considered ethnic minority. We adopted a 90/90/90+ vision. This focus aspired us to work to move 90% and more (included ALL) students to meet or exceed the academic standards at their grade level by the end of each school year.

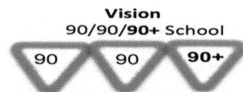

Vision
90/90/**90+** School

90   90   **90+**

Current Reality:
__X__ 90% Free/Reduced
__X__ 90% Ethnic Minority

Achievement Goal:
90% or More Students Will
Meet or Exceed Standards
Spring _____

With a clearly identified vision inscribed in the hearts and minds of staff, we addressed the question... how do we get there? The path for the journey began with school wide goals aligned to the vision.

School Goal:

90% or more of our students will score in the Proficient or Highly Proficient category on weekly, benchmark and end of the year assessments in literacy, mathematics, and science.

Teachers developed strong standard-based lessons and consistently checked students' understandings to meet their daily instructional goals. They used common formative assessments to monitor student learning and the effectiveness of their instructions. Common refers to assessments administered in all classrooms by all teachers at the grade level. Teachers use formative assessments to evaluate student learning in the process toward the goal for the session, day, week and quarter. Information gathered from these assessments provided data that allowed teachers to be able to refine instructions and have an immediate impact on student learning.

Vision sees its work as a continuation of goals. The attainment of one ignites the beginning of another. Vision values the importance of using many forms of data to gauge performance and progress related to the goal. It seeks to move beyond individual parameters to create a culture where team members not only recognize the importance of data but embrace it and thrive on interpreting and utilizing it as a picture for understanding progress. Vision fosters respect, builds trust and promotes accountability through clear and concise communication. It connects horizontally with all individuals to promote an effective team where members understand that formative data is collected regularly to show how the team is progressing towards the goal. It is non-evaluative because it is a point in time used to inform the next steps. Team members understand that where they are, is an okay place to be and it is just not an okay place to stay. When staff members understand where they are, they work to improve the level of effectiveness reflected in their summative results. Each member comprehends the impact of their data on the team's data, the team's data on the school data, the school's data on the current and future lives of the students and on the mission of the school. The presence of this focus makes it easy for each team member to identify where they are in relation to where you are going. The absence of this focus makes it is easy to be satisfied with insubstantial growth.

Teachers enthusiastically work to move forward when they know that where they are is an okay place to be and just not and okay place to stay.

During times when the current reality is out of alignment for reaching the goal, it is easy to yield to the temptation of seeing the goal as too high and conforming to the ordinary. Vision is resolved not to change the goal. Instead, it embraces the goal with firm determination and adjusts or changes the action steps and strategies being employed to advance movement towards the goal.

High expectations support the need for change and celebrate growth that perfects the trajectory. These standards are the force that inspire leaders at all levels to openly delete comments that accept movement outside of the path of the vision.

At the beginning of a third-grade meeting, I displayed the end of the year third grade data and opened with the question, what do you think?

One teacher very honestly responded, "Its growth."

My follow up statement was, one percent is growth. When you look at this growth in relation to your goal and where your team started, is it a meaningful growth? Did it propel your team, to or close to your goal? Was it the thrust you needed to move students through and out of each category?

Team members quickly turned to one another and began to discuss why the growth lacked substance. They identified their areas of strength and their individual and collective next steps. The leader unceasingly works to clarify understandings and help teachers make the connection between formative data and the end of the year summative data. When they see that the information derived from assessments throughout the school year is a predictor for the end of the year summative data, they more clearly understand how each student's success impacts the goal. The complete picture makes the attainment of daily and weekly goals eagerly desirous. Teachers grasp how their individual and collective student data impacts their team and the school. They realize that they are vital links in the chain that binds them together and the work to identify next steps for onward movement towards the goal.

Because where we are is an okay place to be and just not an okay place to stay, we choose to use next steps as opposed to weaknesses. It is very common to hear teachers and leaders throughout the school talking about their next steps. When teachers understand that where they are, is an okay pace to be and just not an okay place to stay, they are at ease discussing where they are and engage and seek support to move forward.

Vision calls to mind the importance of teachers consistently engaging students in their zone of proximal development where they use research-based strategies and practices shown to be effective in increasing learning. When teachers have strong pedagogical knowledge, they support students in mastering skills that are too difficult for them to master on their own or independently but can be mastered with appropriate instruction and guidance.

This chart shows four categories of student performance based on their understanding and application of academic skills. When students make progress, they move over, up or across. Students in the minimally proficient category generally have significant gaps and limited knowledge and skills. The school needs to intervene to effectively support these students. Often a Tier III intervention is included during the school day as a part of the school's programming.

Highly Proficient	Proficient
⭐ MOST DESIRED CATEGORY	⬅ STUDENTS MOVE OVER
Minimally Proficient	**Partially Proficient**
➡ STUDENTS MOVE ACROSS	⬆ STUDENTS MOVE UP

Students in the partially proficient category demonstrate some knowledge and application of the targeted skills. Students in the proficient and highly proficient category generally demonstrate solid academic performance. Often a more rigorous approach is needed to move students across to highly proficient and for highly proficient students to remain in the highly proficient category. Students in the highly proficient category need healthy challenges to continue to grow.

When teachers and students are able to interact with the data and have a wholesome perspective about how it identifies their strengths and next steps, they are energized and empowered to use the waves of information to help them move to their destination of growth and proficiency. They use various forms of specific data to help them make adjustments to lessons, instructional strategies and provide support while learning is happening.

"When it is obvious that the goals cannot be reached, don't adjust the goals, adjust the action steps." –Confucius. To help us understand and operate in the mind frame of this quote, it was introduced, discussed and individually reflected on during a professional development session. It helped build school wide understandings of the significance of clinging to the goal in the presence of challenges. Years later, it continues to speak in the minds of staff and glistens within the fiber of the school. Staff members have adopted the quote and regularly refer to it during conversations, grade level meetings and leadership meetings. It helps us self-correct and keep the focus where the focus should be. In the hands of vision, the use of quotes can be an effective tool to inspire and generate new ideas, provide clarity, reaffirm the purpose and reach beyond the natural boarders to create a frame of reference that makes the invisible visible.

On the journey to the goal, the leader is required to make many serious decisions. Vision helps you stay the narrow course by skillfully sorting through the myriad of choices, waiting, asking and shouting-out to you to be selected. There are dozens of good options. They all have five-star reviews and are supported by research. You personally know many people who are using various ones with a high degree of success. The only thing that separates you from another leader is that you are armed with vision and use knowledge to make informed decisions. This vision licenses you to abandon, ignore and forsake all others because you realize the importance of selecting the products, services and structures that help you excel. Vision allows you to walk in alignment with your high expectations by selecting only the options that align with your goals. It prompts you to intentionally select those practices and resources that point you towards your desired outcomes. All others, regardless of how good they appear to be, if selected, will get in the way of the best. Vision recognizes that good and best are competing for the same space.

1	2	3	4	GOAL	1	2	3	4	GOAL
↘	↗	→	↙	→	●	●	◉	●	●
Circle the BEST choice.					Circle the BEST choice.				
Justify your response.					Justify your response.				

Photographers search for the perfect backdrop to enhance the look of their photographs because they understand that the type of backdrop they use can seriously affect the quality and clarity of the photo or portrait. A carefully selected backdrop will accurately depict the mood and personality the photographer seeks to create. Like the photographer, the leader must use the best possible backdrop to keep attention focused on the vision. When the goal of the organization is the backdrop for data conversations, the momentum shifts into a gear for success. The leader uses the backdrop to respectfully question and even refute statements in the foreground that do not coordinate with the goals.

"They did not move because they were so low. I tried hard, but they did not get any help at home. We did good, a little better than last year."

Statements of this nature, when allowed to go unchecked, will affect the clarity of the vision. Consistently using the goal as the backdrop places the emphasis on high expectations and points all others in the direction of the vision. It transforms the organization by building collective commitment that expands ownership and builds leadership capacity. The leader's backdrop like that of a photographer will seriously affect the quality and clarity of the outcomes. The image the leader creates will allow others to clearly see and align with the message. Knowing your vision and identifying your backdrop is critical. All other steps spring from this foundation.

What backdrop are your expectations reflected on?

After viewing her data and realizing that 60% of her students did not meet their goals, the teacher approached me with a list of five students and the number of days they had been absent. She pointed to one student who had scored in the minimally proficient category and commented that he has been absent for 40 days. My question was, how many days has he been present? Following up with, what support did he receive when he was here? Vision arms you with the power necessary to be ready with a backdrop that depicts the mood you wish to create. The sense of urgency for reaching the goal inspires leaders to help others understand the need to give up every excuse and push towards the goal. When vision is the backdrop for all conversations, it creates an image that reflects important elements of the organization. The utilization of every moment to combat the enemy of excuses that threatens high expectations is not just important, it is absolutely necessary.

What do you allow, communicate, expect and celebrate?

An observation in a school pamphlet read, "Now we are moving into the next phase, which is putting the emphasis and intentionality into student academic success. We will remember, we are not doing this for a test score, but to give our kids every opportunity they deserve."

A leader with a vision for student success understands that what happens in the schools affects students' lives. They further understand that it is the responsibility and goal of the school to engage students in high levels of learning that increase confidence, improve academic performance and equip them to master grade-level standards. When students gain the knowledge and skills needed to master these standards they will pass the test. The goal is to provide instructions that help students learn and achieve academic success. Learning equips students to pass the test. Passing the test provides evidence that student learning has occurred.

The test score is the result, the natural outcome of learning and not the reason to learn.

Vision sees no real difference in learning and passing the test. Vision allows the leader to further see that it is important to help students and adults understand the nature and purpose of assessments. When students understand that assessment is a natural part of life, they have acquired an important building block. Helping students to learn the skills and processes, they will need to take an assessment strengthens their confidence and clarifies their understanding of the role of the assessment. Learning empowers students to succeed on grade level assessments, college entrance exams and post-graduate career exams. The parent, teacher, administrator, family member or friend who helps the student develop a wholesome mind set towards taking an assessment has a healthy and lofty vision for the child.

| True/False | Instruction + Learning = Proficiency (Test Scores) |
| True/False | Learning = Passing the Test |

What connections do you see between learning and the test score?

On the freeway of thought in any area of life, vision looks ahead. It knows when and how to check its personal GPS, navigate around roadblocks of negativity and keep right on towards the goal.

One phlebotomist attempted to draw blood and when she failed to locate the vein on the first attempt, she asked, "Do they have trouble finding your veins?"

When the second attempt was unsuccessful, she repeated the question, and sought someone else to take over the procedure.

The second phlebotomist entered the room, examined the arms of the patient and said, "You are my friend, I see you."

When she stuck the needle into the arm, she said, "Come on, I see you."

The words of the second phlebotomist were not spoken to the patient. Why do you think these words were spoken and how do the two individuals differ?

How did the personal data within each phlebotomist inspire the thinking, therefore the outcome?
Reflections:

Vision interrupts, speaks and clarifies to support leadership and all areas of life.

Vision does not recognize or know failure. It lights the candle of hope and anticipation as it stretches to achieve its created image. When we activate vision, embrace high expectations and allow it to move us beyond challenges, we enter into a new dimension of personal possibilities.

What is the connection between mental data and your vision?
Reflections :

Section Three

Words

The Echo of Vision

Words repeated again and again resonate to reflect the voice of the speaker.

Several years ago, an employee in district leadership began sending emails to teachers and administrators with headings such as: Dear Amazing Teachers, Awesome Administrators. Others throughout the district quickly adopted this practice. Within a short period of time, emails addressing staff as terrific, fantastic and awesome became the norm. Words of this nature are pleasing to the ears, feelings and mind. Whereas, it is important to appreciate those with whom we live and work, individuals who are seriously accountable for the growth and development of others; use every opportunity to speak words of encouragement that convey direction, affirmation and clarity. Addressing individuals or groups as treasure finders, committed, unique and talented, united team and effective team recognize the efforts and achievements of the staff as a part of the big picture of the organization. Leaders and individuals put their adjectives to work by aligning them with specific direction, focus or outcomes. They use carefully selected descriptive words or phrases as opportunities to appreciate individuals or groups for their specific efforts in connection with the goal. Vision prompts leaders to avoid idol words and cling to high expectations in all situations.

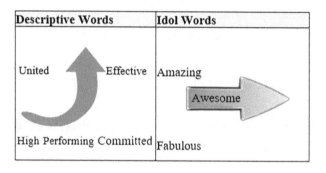

Descriptive Words	Idol Words
United Effective	Amazing
	Awesome
High Performing Committed	Fabulous

Leaders with vision understand that words are more than sounds formed as air passes through the larynx. They know that kind words are powerful creative forces and have the potential to move the team forward.

"Words can light fires in the minds of men." — Patrick Rothfuss, *The Name of the Wind.*

Leaders work to create a common language that flows to and among all members of the school. Language that is specific, purposeful, confirming, directional and works to achieve the vision captured by the leader. The expectations of leaders conveyed through formal and casual use of words are transmissible to other members within the organization thorough direct and indirect contact. These transmissions help to create one language and inspire others to work in the spirit of oneness to accomplish what they purpose.

Leaders use every opportunity to communicate focus and build vision for the mission. The words of the leader carry energy and substance and have the capacity to influence. The leader ensures that carefully selected words create a straight line to the vision.

Included, here are a few examples of how simple messages sent to staff can express appreciation and intentionally influence thinking while they point to purpose and vision. The leader can be very creative in the frequency and the nature of the messages.

This welcoming message that clarifies expectations was sent to staff a few days before the start of the new school year.

Welcome back new and returning staff,

In August, a new group of students will walk onto our campus and through the door to your classroom. Their parents send them in hopes that the learning opportunities and experiences they receive, will dramatically enhance their chances of success. The start of this school year provides a fresh opportunity for you to facilitate instructions that pushes each student to high levels of learning and to their goals. May your end of the year data tell us that this has been the best year yet for you, your students, your team and our school!

Looking forward to supporting you as we support our students.

The leader uses words to connect with the staff and to communicate care and concern. This message was sent to the staff the day the school closed for winter break.

To our precious staff,

May this holiday season and the days to come throughout the new year present to you and your family, the experience of deeper love for one another, joy in being together, and peace in knowing you are not alone.

You are uniquely you and you are valued for contributions to our school that only you can make. Thank you for all that you do. **Happy Holidays!**

This message was sent the evening prior to the staff's return from winter break.

Good evening,

I hope this email finds you well and winding down a joyous holiday break! Looking forward to continuing the work with renewed energy and focus.

See you tomorrow.

How does the leader's word choice differ in the memos to the staff before and after the winter break?

What does the leader seek to convey through this message to the staff?

Happy Return!

It is my hope that you have experienced a restful and enjoyable spring break. I believe you are returning with renewed energy, a clear focus and a deeper commitment to our students' success. Let's finish strong and make this the year of the highest student buy-in and highest academic gains in our school's history as recorded in our end of the year results.

Thank you for defending your position and holding up the arms of our school. You are appreciated and valued!

The visionary leader understands that words powerfully impact the organization. They create a picture of who the leader is and what the leader desires for the school. Words help others identify what the leader expects, values and celebrates. Vision realizes that words release a powerful force with endless echoes. Because others often rise to the expectations of the leader, the leader constructively connects with this power by tailoring words to build commitment and create lasting impressions.

"Handle them carefully, for words have more power than atom bombs." –Pearl Strachan Hurd.

Vision sees the organization through the eyes of the gardener. It knows that within each small seed is the capacity for that seed to produce more of its kind. Vision carefully selects words that prepare the soil of the mind. Words plant seeds. Words are the fertilizer, food and water needed for adequate nourishment. Words seep deep into the mental soil and cause the seeds to germinate and optimize the quantity and quality of the crop. Words cultivate the mind, nurture the seeds and call them forth. Vision realizes that healthy things grow towards their goal. Therefore, it continually sends out its words, then waits and watches for signs of healthy vegetation.

Think of the school or your sphere of influence as a garden. Ask yourself, how is my garden growing? What type seeds have I planted? What do I cultivate? Vision concludes that the school, the garden, is not about you. Yet, it is everything about you. It is about how do you prepare your soil, select your seeds, cultivate, and nurture your seeds. Are you patiently watching for healthy vegetation? It is about how the leader guards and protects the vision to keep it clear, alive and healthy so that it takes root and lives among the people. It is about the vision's ability to guard and protect itself so that the capacity to reproduce itself is exponentially enhanced within the organization.

Teachers are expected to electronically submit lesson plans by Monday morning. After receiving each teacher's lesson plan, the leader acknowledges receipt to each teacher by sending an empowering message.

Lesson Plan Comments	
Date	Thank you! May you be flanked with kindness throughout the week as you lead your students to mastery.
Date	Thank you! You are a bright light in the lives of the students. May you be surrounded with encouragement as you lead your students to mastery.
Date	Thank you! Our students grow socially and academically because of you. May all your wishes and the wishes of those you love come true as you lead your students to mastery.

Consider the power within your words. How do you utilize that power?
Reflections:

Leaders who have watched the words planted in the fertile garden soil grow into beautiful flowers know that pruning is necessary to improve the overall beauty. Pruning removes the part of the plant that is no longer useful. The skilful leader knows when and how to prune each one to prevent the spread of disease and improve the overall health of the garden. Leaders understand which words and actions are needed to remove doubt, unbelief and resistance that threaten the health of the organization. The leader recognizes the beauty and greatness within each individual and intentionally engages in conversations and actions to help people work together. This helps create a fusion that inspires the team to stay the narrow course and become more effective. Use your words to intentionally light an eternal flame of unity, focus and direction that will continuously burn within the hearts, minds and walls of the school. They will call the people to new heights, new depths and new dimensions of their roles.

How are you cultivating your garden?
Reflections:

Section Four

Section 1.2.1

Unity
The Inclusiveness of Vision

Unity *ushers in an environment where everyone feels valued, connected to one another and to achieving the goals.*

After reading a paragraph the school leader had written to the staff, where five out of five sentences began with I, the following questions came to mind. Is there a singular or collective focus? Will these words inspire ownership? Is this an opinion piece? Many leaders frequently use I, me or my when conversing with or addressing staff, while other leaders choose we or our to project unity. Vision rejects I did, I learned, I want, I will, I know and chooses to operate in the language of we did, we learned, we want, we will and we know to inspire and help members see themselves working in partnership with their teammates to produce a quality outcome.

Vision understands that words are strong and make robust impressions within the organization. The leader with vision is committed to team and consistently uses we or our to help form, promote and sustain the team.

The language of the leader has the ability to reproduce the status quo or to produce a spirit of unity and exceptional quality and services. This language often becomes embedded within the subconscious and affects the feelings and behaviors of team members. Frequently, without thinking, others adopt the words of the leader and communicate the same level of ownership.

Vision facilitates the simple practice of speaking in a united voice of we and our to increase harmony and buy-in for success. This voice shapes the culture within the workplace often without members realizing that it is being shaped. The we, our leader, fosters a team that sees and discusses their efforts and results in a collective voice. Maintaining this type of environment requires continuous focus and nurturing because many individuals have formed the habit of operating from the I and my perspective. Vision does not assume everyone understands the concept. The leader's consistent use of we is critical. When this is coupled with simple training that addresses the 'we' focus and the reason for this focus, it will create a chain reaction throughout the school.

The school staff engaged in discussions and conversations to help discern the difference between I, me, we and our. Observational notes taken during professional development sessions provided feedback to coaches that helped them broaden their perspectives and be able to model this concept throughout the school. The benefits of this focus were many. As a team, we grew to understand that we were connected to one another and our work was interdependent. Our words reflected this connection. Consequently, staff freely and regularly reached out to others to seek support and to provide support. It was not unusual to walk through a classroom and see another classroom teacher modeling a strategy in a colleague's classroom or observing a colleague's lesson. This practice continues to reproduce 'we' and 'our' mind-sets.

Earlier in our school development process, the words below could have been observed on chart paper in a leadership meeting with teacher leaders or in a professional development session.

They were used to develop understanding and inspire while revealing the power and connectivity words convey.

Count your I's. Divide them by the total and subtract
1 from the quotient.

Throughout our school we have developed the we and our climate. The leadership team, grade level leaders, coaches, teachers and other staff talk about our goals, our work, our students, our results and our school. It is common for staff to envision themselves as a part of a team and speak with a shared sense of mission and a collective focus. What does this look like? What are the benefits?

The adoption of the we-our mind set creates a shift from working in isolation and moves individuals to the realization that they are not alone and they are a part of a team. This mind set introduces one to the vastness of resources available under the umbrella of team. Some of the most beneficial thought patterns include the following: I am a part of a team surrounded by support. We help one another achieve their goals. Our team plans and works together. We help all team members develop their full potential. Our overall success is defined by the success of each student. We work to develop our individual and collective efficacy where we know that alone and as a team, we have the knowledge and influence necessary to move our students to mastery. Every student is our responsibility. We will continually examine what we have done, identity what needs to be done and explore options for our next steps. All minds, hearts and hands are committed to the work to achieve the desired outcomes. As the organization develops ownership and begins to operate in the we-our mind set, it comes to appreciate the power deposited in the garden of the mind to produce beautiful bouquets of potential.

The leader's interaction with vision is continually present. At frequent intervals the leader uses reflection to clarify and confirm thoughts, decision or actions. Vision guides the leader's reflection and provides these and many other prompts relevant to the work:

- What do I know?
- What do I want for the school?
- How will I begin?

Whereas the use of I in the leader's reflection, might seem contradictory to the we and our mind set; it is not. The leaders' clear understanding of where they are going is necessary before they can kindle and keep aglow the fire of courage and high expectations that direct others to a place of excellence. Successful leadership is noted in its ability to see where it is going and to effectively communicate in a manner that allows others to see and come.

Section Five

Professional Development
The Empowerment of Vision

Professional development supplies the tools and resources employees need to be effective within their areas of responsibility.

Vision is the solid foundation on which the team is built. It is the backdrop on which the team views challenges and creates beautiful portraits of success. The vastness of vision guides the team through the shallow thinking and launches it into deep understanding. It empowers the staff to generate their own response to this question, do we have to do this? The leader has the responsibility and the charge of making the vision crystal clear so that every member in the organization knows and understands why they do what they do. The leader makes the vision plain through the development of an action plan with action steps that include a clearly defined professional development plan. The professional development plan addresses the current needs of the organization. It includes desired outcomes that help team members understand the benefits of specific trainings and evidence of completion. The professional development plan serves as a compass that inspires motivation and builds momentum for advancing toward the goals.

Upon beginning my tenure as principal, I had a desire to honor the legacy and honor the people, while shaping the culture. Student learning data, school progress data, demographic data and perception data revealed the need to develop characteristics, structures and processes to help our students learn at high levels. There was a need to develop a plan to engage the staff in professional development to support us in these efforts. A learning team was identified at the beginning of the second year. This team engaged in a year-long professional development study of the Effective Schools Research by Larry Lazotte which was specifically aligned to our next steps. The study involved four off campus sessions that met throughout the year. We understood that these characteristics correlated with student success. So, we did not look at how far away we were from each characteristic; instead, we identified action steps we could take to involve the staff, create a shared sense of purpose and begin to implement this.

At the end of each learning session, the team was inspired to move forward with a sense of urgency. We planned for how we would rollout the information to other staff members and include them in the new learning to build commitment to the vision and set goals. The learning team facilitated professional development and was a catalyst in involving the staff. School-wide teams were formed. The teams set school-wide goals and grade-level teams set grade-level goals aligned to the school goals. We developed our core values and shared commitments.

By the end of that year, a clear and definite framework was developing. This intentional professional development was a pivotal point in the school's history. It inspired teachers and began a process of empowerment whereby they understood the rationale for engaging in the work. Unrelentingly communicating the vision and pointing to the vision as the rationale for the work we engaged in and for what we discontinued created a spirit of perseverance and high expectations. The leadership team, grade level teams and staff worked with a clear focus and shared commitment to students learning. The process included both certified and classified staff.

Acquired knowledge and the strengthening of professional skills pointed the staff to a higher level of vision. A new culture was forming and a climate of trust and learning was developing. The staff was embracing action steps that included a more definite and specific focus on academic, social and emotional success for each student. The vision was unfolding in the hearts of teachers, coaches and administrators. They were seeing themselves as a team united to achieve this mission. As the work continued, the staff was engaged in understanding educational research specific to the current needs and concerns of the school.

The professional development model where the principal learned alongside the staff and everyone worked to implement with a sense of urgency had been very successful and therefore, we continued this model. During the summers, we learned together and planned for instructions to address the needs of the students. To build shared knowledge aligned to our goals, we used educational consultants and the leadership team to facilitate during Thursday professional development sessions. Because the professional development was specifically aligned to our next steps, the teachers had a vision for how it impacted their practice and they wanted to implement those right away. They agreed that they would all begin implementing these steps the Monday following the professional development session. In many cases, teachers began the next day.

Staff members understand that vision is powerful and binds them together in philosophy and in practice. It causes them to see beyond circumstances and set new standards for themselves and their community. Below is an aspirational description of what the school desires to become. It shows three steps that are necessary for the school to move towards the vision. Each step is supported by professional development. Fidelity identifies areas in which the staff desires strict adherence to. Beliefs express the confidence that staff and students have in the value of hard work.

The First Best Instruction list involves strategies that will be used to promote student learning. This visual serves as a guide for the course of action. It illuminates their route and points out professional development markers necessary to reach each designated point.

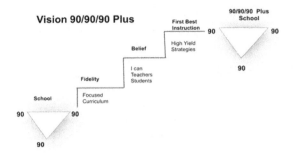

Created by Bobbie Blair

Vision knows the way to the goal. It works in the leader to see the way and go the way. It informs the leader of the need for a strong and diversified professional development plan that under girds the skills and ability levels of each staff with the goal of improving instruction in every classroom. Vision shifts the focus from one size fits all professional development models to a model that is tailored so that teachers can get the support they need to advance them to their next level.

To develop the confidence, knowledge and skills needed to address students' learning challenges, the staff embraced professional development in various forms during the workday. Early release Thursdays provided opportunities to tailor professional development to the current needs and interest. Additionally, there were many opportunities to support previous learning and embed new learning. The workday included different ways to support teachers at all levels of growth and development. This support for learning emerged as a solid structure to strengthen the school and move it forward.

Type of Support	Focus/Agenda Menu	Participants
Leadership Meetings	Mini Lessons, Data, Current Reality, Discussions, Next Steps, Reflections	Leadership Team (Open to All Staff)
Grade Level Meetings	Data, Student Work Samples, Understanding Academic Standards, Planning Instruction for Mastery of Standards: What Does Mastery Look Like? Checking for Understanding, Assessment, Next Steps Social, Emotional Learning Needs	Grade Level Team Members, Coaches, Administrator(s) Special Request: School Counselor, School Psychologist
Teacher Observe Teacher	Teacher Determines Focus: Based of Teacher's Interest or Next Steps	Teacher, Coach or Admin if Whisper Coaching is Desired
Teacher Model for Teacher	Teacher Determines Focus: Based on Teacher's Interest or Next Steps	Teacher
Discussions/Study Groups	Data, Next Steps, Teacher Interest	Teacher, Coaches, Admin
Coaching	Data, Next Steps, Teacher Interest	Coaches, Admin
Observations/Feedback	Data, Next Steps, Teacher Interest	Coaches, Admin
Early Release Thursdays	Data, Next Steps: Whole Group or Differentiated Sessions	All Certified Staff
Off-Site Learning Sessions	Designated Topics	Designated Staff
Classified Staff	Data, Next Steps,	Classified Staff

This professional development model formed around the premise that the staff had the freedom to make mistakes and practice with support, but without judgement. It was created and maintained with the involvement of the staff. Vision places people at the heart of the work and views the success of professional development as a continuous process that reaches its greatest impact when the teacher's voice is valued. The model that was birthed with the teacher input, for teacher effectiveness and by teacher leadership proved to be powerful in fostering teacher development and building leadership capacity. Because the classroom teacher is the principle learner in school wide professional development, that voice is present in the planning, implementation and monitoring of professional development.

Professional Development feedback is requested at the end of the learning session as a means of evaluating the effectiveness of the session, identifying follow-up support the teacher needs and to capture the teacher's voice. Below is an example of a simple feedback form created for this purpose.

Professional Development Feedback Form	
Teacher:	Grade: Date:
Session Target:	Success Criteria:
Rate your current level of understanding in relation to the session target.	Surface, Deep, Transfer
Rate your current level of understanding in relation to the success criteria.	Surface, Deep, Transfer
What questions do you have?	
What support do you need?	
List possible days/times this support can be provided.	
Think about today's PD, identify the **Strengths** and **Next Steps**.	
Strengths:	Next Steps:
Comments:	

Vision guides the leader to understand that training is the most powerful weapon that can be used to change the level of effectiveness of each employee, the level of learning for each student and thus change the school. Vision understands that professional development needs to be ongoing, timely and differentiated for teachers so it addresses where each teacher is, so they can move to the next level. Below is an example of the gradual release model of support for teachers. It focuses on the idea that each teacher gets the support needed to help them become independent. The degree of support is increased or decreased based on the need of the teacher.

This chart shows three basic levels of support provided for teachers. The most support is provided at Level A and the least amount of support is provided at Level C. The support is fluid to meet the current needs of the teacher. Teachers can move in and out of levels. Any teacher may request support with planning, model or whisper coach at any time. Teachers understand that together we work to meet the goal for high levels of learning in each classroom.

Model for During the Day Job Embedded PD				
Levels.of.Support	Day 1	Day 2	Day 3	Day 4
Level A				
Support: Coach	Plan/Model Debrief	Model/ Team Teach/ Debrief	Team Teach/ Whisper Coach/ Feedback	Observe/ Feedback ↻
Support: Admin	Provide Walk Through Feedback, Model, Whisper Coach as Needed			
Level B				
Support: Coach	Team Teach/ Whisper Coach/ Debrief	Observe/ Whisper Coach/	Observe/Feedback	↻
Support: Admin	Provide Walk Through Feedback, Model, Whisper Coach as Needed			
Level C				
Support: Coach	Observe/ Feedback	Observe/ Feedback		↻
Support: Admin	Provide Walk Through Feedback, Model, Whisper Coach as Needed			
*PD: Professional Development	↻ Any part of the process is repeated as needed			

Vision realizes the importance of streamlining professional development so that it is specific, targeted and connects to the existing goals of the organization. It should not necessarily widen the focus, but deepen the focus. The leadership team supports teachers to ensure that the vision for the professional development is evident as teachers in every classroom become proficient in the utilization of skills, strategies or procedures targeted by the professional development.

Following the learning session, the coaches and administrators consistently work to job embedded and differentiated professional development. To meet the needs of individual teachers and grade level teams, coaches and administrators used the gradual release model to support the new learning through modeling, team teaching, whisper coaching, observation and feedback.

Vision identifies professional development as a foundational building block with the power to both initiate and sustain the growth and development of the organization. The leader with vision engages staff in training to improve skills that lead to increased student learning results.

Professional development is the bridge of transformation that took teachers from new and novice to returning and highly effective. It eased doubts, erased fears and encouraged questions and change that led to growth and proficiency. It was the foundation on which the progress was initiated and must be the cycle for sustaining continuous improvement.

Below is a section of the professional development agenda that shows the session target and the success criteria. The session target is the overall objective for the session. It identifies what the participants are expected to learn. It is in alignment with the school goals which are based on various forms of student learning data. The success criteria identify skills, strategies and understanding needed for participants to demonstrate mastery of the session target.

Date/Topics/Audience	Session.Target/Success Criteria
Date: 00/00/00	**Target:** I will be able to answer the question: What do my students need to be able to do to demonstrate the characteristics of visible learners? **Success Criteria:** I will know I have it when I can **Surface Level:**
Visible Learner Part 1	
Introducing the Visible Learner	• Identify what research says students need to be able to do to be visible learners **Deep Level:** • Understand the characteristics of visible learners I want my students to exhibit.
Whole Group: **Grades: K-5**	• Identify where I am and see where I need to go. **Transfer Level:** • Develop visible learners

A district-wide focus on visible learning provided training and meaningful information for deepening the school focus. System-wide training created a common language and a common focus within our school. Vision helps the leader see the importance of working in alignment with district initiatives and goals. The leader interacts and communicates with the school staff in a manner that helps them to see and understand their connection to the larger outside community of the school district. They understand that their work as a part of the district-wide community mirrors their work in the school community. The effectiveness of each classroom directly impacts the school and the lives of their students. Likewise, the success of the school in achieving its goals impacts the effectiveness of the school district and affects the lives of students within the larger community.

Within our school, we understand that members of the organization are thoroughly connected in vision, purpose and the commitment to the work. The same vision and commitments that outlines a path to student success and attaches us to one another, student by student, classroom by classroom and grade level by grade level is the same vision that links us to the school district, the state, nation and world. An infinite number of invisible threads expand our world by connecting our work to the rest of humanity. 'We are one,' in partnership with one another to ensure a better world.

"We don't accomplish anything in this world alone... and whatever happens is the result of the whole tapestry of one's life and all the weavings of individual treads from one to another that creates something." –Sandra Day O'Connor.

Section Six

Feedback
The Voice of Vision

Openly expressed feedback creates a natural and distinctive tone within the organization.

My early years as principal were met with strong resistance to feedback. The staff was negative and vehemently opposed to feedback because they saw it as an invasion of their privacy, 'negative criticism', and a threat to their jobs. Vision does not accept where it is. Instead, it sees what it can become. Vision acknowledged the need to move, to move quickly and in a spirit that built up and empowered others. Information and research regarding feedback was continually shared with staff. Questions were answered and there were ongoing open discussions and many opportunities for conversations. The rationale for feedback was presented, explained and discussed. Feedback was the talk of the school. Recognizing the enormous potential possessed by each individual, vision was relentless in its efforts to support, teach, model and help the staff understand the role of feedback in the continuous school improvement process.

Vision operates in the spirit of transparency regarding the expectations for each member of the team. It guides the leader to a level of understanding that reveals the importance of scheduling ample time at the start of the school year to revisit administrative norms and teach policies, procedures and structure regarding the operation of the school. The Welcome Back Session is a time for teaching the staff how they are expected to operate within the school environment.

Below are administrative norms and session objectives that were repeatedly used to clarify each employee's understanding of their role in the organization. This information is shared in this section, because this process is vital to creating understandings that nurture and support the mind-sets needed to inspire openness to change. Vision strategically lays every building block to form a solid foundation.

Welcome Back Orientation
Administrative Norms
1. We are respectful of others. If conflict arises, we resolve it quickly and respectfully. 2. We collaborate with team members and other members of the school community to benefit students and for the good of the school. 3. We maximize time on task for all students in all classrooms at all times. 4. We accept feedback as a gift, ask clarifying questions, reflect and revise our practice.
Policies and Procedures Session Objective By the end of this session, I will be knowledgeable of practices, procedures, structures and expectations on the School Campus and understand my role as a member of the This Team.
Evaluation Session Objective By the end of this session, I will understand the observation cycle and how I will be evaluated
Note: Administrative norms are identified by administrators because they are believed to be vital and non-negotiable. The staff closest to the work takes the lead in identifying norms for professional development, grade level meeting and other areas as needed.

Vision invokes listening. It causes the leader to process what is heard in line with the goals and moves to timely link clarity, sincerity, accountability and feedback to the desired end of the year results for each staff member. The leader unquestionably understands that the purpose of walk-through observations is to improve student learning. Vision consistently communicates that where you are is an okay pace to be and just not an okay place to stay. The evaluation continuum and the evaluation cycle were visuals created and used to help the staff understand that feedback was support designed to help them improve their practice. Over time, these supports linked with the constant message of accountability, coupled with trust and delivered in a non-threatening manner broke down the walls of fear and distrust. As the staff began to see clearly through new lens, they began to feel the air of support and unity. This process transformed the campus from resisting feedback to requesting feedback.

Each year during the Evaluation Section of the Welcome Back Orientation Agenda, the evaluation goal is introduced. Staff members understand that the purpose of evaluation is to improve their performance and help them achieve effectiveness in their classroom or assigned area. The evaluation continuum and the observation cycle were presented as a tool to enable the staff to see that all stages are important. Engaging in each stage helps the staff member move forward and end in a happy place.

The evaluation continuum gives an overall picture of the important stages that lead to continuous teacher development.

Evaluation Continuum					I am here! ☺	
Classroom Walk Through	Feedback	Reflection	Support and/or Collective Inquiry	Adjust Practice	Effective or Highly Effective Rating	☺

The observation cycle helped staff understand that when timely and specific feedback is given, they have the responsibility to act. The staff members openly responded by seeking support to move them from where they were to where they wanted to be.

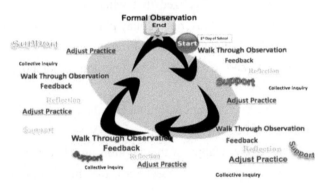

Observation Cycle

The observation cycle begins on the first day. Teachers understand and welcome the early intervention. The observation cycle shows the menu of options available to the teacher following the feedback. Teachers take the lead in solidifying and refining their practices. They select the support they need. Teachers may ask clarifying questions, seek support from coaches, administrators, colleagues, or engage in a type of study and then adjust their practice. Feedback to the teacher included strengths and next steps for that purpose. The objective is for future walk-through feedback to capture the progress the teachers have made towards their next steps. Walk through feedback forms were initially shared with the staff and their questions were addressed prior to using the forms. The goal of administrators and coaches was to support each teacher in perfecting their practice to increase student learning outcomes in their classroom and assist the teacher in moving to the Effective or Highly Effective category at the end of the year evaluation.

As this movement occurs, the benefits become wide spread affecting the teacher, students, school and community. The staff members understood and accepted their responsibility. They realized that where they were was an okay place to be and just not an okay place to stay. Therefore, they readily engaged in differentiated professional development and welcomed new learning to support their next steps.

Both the evaluation continuum and the observation cycle show the staff ending in a happy place. Vision does not start out to be happy. Happy is the emotion unveiled when hard work, commitment and respect form the three-strand chord that upholds the organization through all phases of development.

Sometimes you work hard with no observable evidence. In the heart of a leader, vision creates an indelible image and the drive to leap over obstacles that appear static to chase that image with all of your might. Vision knows that the image it has captured is the guiding force that will stimulate an organization or group at rest and will turn around one moving in the wrong direction. Vision engages strategies that act as a rudder to steer hearts and minds, brings people together, synergizes them and keeps them living in the realm of expectancy. The leader utilizes feedback, a condition of learning that promotes the greatest degree of change, to move beyond the shallow banks of we will try and we hope so into the deep waters of we can and we will.

Feedback has the potential to change undesirable practices, refine developing practices and enrich effective practices. When given regularly and with clear expectations, but in a non-threatening manner, feedback achieves the greatest degree of effectiveness. Feedback to the employee should be a continuous flow of information that is clear enough to be implemented and specific enough to positively impact one's practice. Staff should see feedback as their helping hand and understand their responsibility as the receiver of feedback.

Below is a walkthrough form that captures feedback to a teacher following a Thursday professional development session. The strengths identified that the teacher has mastered an important focus of a previous professional development session. The next steps identified specific areas the teacher needed to target.

Walk Through Observation Feedback Form
Teacher: A   **Grade:** 5th   **Time:** 8:50 9:15 **Date:**   00/00/00**Administrator:**
Strengths:
1. Explicit model of metacognitive strategies to promote students' understanding of main idea.
Next Steps:
2. How do you promote student to student interactions (Increase opportunities for meaningful student talk)?   3. Help students understand that you expect all students to engage during choral reading (Ten students actively reading).   4. Two out of 16 students knew what they were learning. Zero students knew where they were in their learning. Ensure that all students know what they are learning, where they are in their learning and what they need to learn next.

Below is a walkthrough form that captures feedback in the same classroom two weeks after the first feedback was given to the teacher. The time period allowed the teacher time to seek support, practice, make and refine mistakes without judgement. All forms of support must be aimed at student outcomes. The observations must be factual and free of negative judgement. The ☺ could be considered judgement, however it was used to confirm the teacher's positive progress. The ☺ was used only to capture strong positive movement. It was welcomed by the staff.

Walk Through Observation Feedback Form			
Teacher: A Grade:		**Time:** 9:00–9:15	**Date:** Two Weeks Later

Administrator:

Strengths:

1. Three opportunities for students to engage in timely and meaningful discussions with shoulder partner and one opportunity for table group discussions. Students turned directly to partner when requested. ☺
3. Teacher: "I am looking to see that everyone is reading and listening to hear all voices."
This statement sent a clear expectation to students. They responded to your expectation by participating in choral reading (27/27). Two students (#8 and #14) were attempting to follow along although they were experiencing difficulty. Continue this practice. ☺
2. Eight out of ten students identified what they were learning. Six students identified where they were in their learning. Five students identified they were at surface, deep or transfer and explained why (S: I can identify nonliteral language. D: I can tell the difference between literal and nonliteral language. T: I can describe how nonliteral language affects what I think about the characters). All five students identified where they would go to next. ☺

Next Steps:

1. Continue to provide opportunities for students to engage in meaningful elaborate discussions. Teach students how to listen and add on to what another student said by using (agree because, I agree and would like to add, I disagree because). Teach students to question.

Continue to develop visible learners by helping all students consistently articulate their understanding of what they are learning and what they will learn next.

Why do you think this feedback was given?

Reflections:

Below is an example of a weekly data report submitted by a third-grade teacher. It shows the name and percentage of students who scored in each of the performance categories.

Weekly Data Report				Date:
	Teacher: B	Grade: Content Area:		
Highly Proficient 100–90%	(21%)	Proficient 89–70%		(43%)
Student #1	Student #4	Student #1	Student #5	Student #9
Student #2	Student #5	Student #2	Student #6	Student #10
Student #3	Student #6	Student #3	Student #7	Student #11
		Student #4	Student #8	Student #12
Minimally Proficient: 59% or Below.	11%	Partially Proficient 69 60%		(18%)
37–49%	50–59%	Student #1		Student #4
Student #1	Student #1	Student #2		Student #5
	Student #2	Student #3		
Absent: Student #27, Student # 28 (07%)				

Weekly data reports are submitted by each teacher on Friday afternoon or prior to 8:00 a.m. on Monday morning. The principal provides data feedback to each teacher and uses the data report to guide administrative walkthroughs for the week. The data report is also used by coaches to help provide targeted coaching support.

The principal uses a quick turn-around window for providing feedback to each teacher. The feedback is recorded on the weekly data feedback form and emailed to each teacher following the receipt of their weekly data report.

Weekly Data Feedback		
Teacher: B	Grade: Content Area:	Date

Goal is Highly Proficient/Proficient: 64% are on target.
What part of the success criteria do the proficient students need to master to move to highly proficient?

Partially Proficient: 18% approaching the target.
What part of the success criteria do these students not understand? What errors are they making?
Review "Next Steps" from walk through feedback forms.

Minimally Proficient: 11%
The three students in minimally proficient made growth from last week. Continue checking their understanding of the success criteria and providing Tier Two intervention as needed.

Note: Student #27 and #28 absent this week were absent last week. Contact family and communicate vision for the students. Involve the counselor as needed to help students maintain regular attendance.

Thank you for submitting your data! Keep Pushing!

The principal uses a variety of forms to provide meaningful feedback to staff. Below is a section of another copy of timely and specific feedback the principal provided a teacher following a professional development session.

Teacher: C	Grade:	Time: 9:54–10:10	Date: 00/00/00	Administrator:
	Teacher: Grade: Time:		Date: Admin:	

Upon entering the classroom, the teacher was: engaging students in differentiated and small group-explicit math instruction

Upon entering the classroom, the students were: working independently, with partners and in a small group with the teacher.

Number and Operation – Fractions	5. NF.A. 1

Lesson Target: I can add and subtract fractions with unlike denominators including mixed numbers.

Success Criteria: I will know I have it when I can:

Surface: I can us visual models to: Add and subtract fractions with unlike denominators including mixed numbers by: Step 1: Replacing given fractions with equivalent fractions with like denominators Step 2: Add or subtract to produce a sum or difference of fractions with like denominators	**Deep:** I can without the use of visual models: Add and subtract fractions with unlike denominators including mixed numbers by: Step 1: Replacing given fractions with equivalent fractions with like denominators Step 2: Add or subtract to produce a sum or difference of fractions with like denominators	**Transfer:** I can without the use of visual models: Add and subtract fractions with unlike denominators including mixed numbers by: Step 1: Explain how to replace given fractions with equivalent fractions with like denominators Step 2: Explain how to add or subtract to produce a sum or difference of fractions with like denominators Step 3: Justify why a sum or difference is correct or incorrect
What are you learning?	**Where are you in your learning?**	**What will you learn next?**
1. How to add and subtract fractions	1. Surface: Using the manipulatives for mixed numbers	1. Deep: Without manipulatives
2. How to add and subtract fractions	2. Deep: Understand #1 and 2	2. Need to be able to explain my work
3. How to add and subtract fractions	3. Deep: Step 1 and 2. Need help with mixed numbers	
4. How to add and subtract fractions	4. Transfer: I am able to explain	4. To interpret and solve word problems
Responses 4 out of 4	Responses 4 out of 4	Responses 4 out of 4

Strengths:

1. Evidence of content and academic vocabulary use by students.
2. Evidence of interactive classroom environment. Students work with partners and explain their thinking.
3. All four of the students asked knew: what they are learning, where they are in their learning and what they will learn next.
4. Success criteria written from surface, deep, transfer.

☺ Continue all of these practices

Next Steps:

1. Continue to refer to the target throughout the lesson, check students' understandings of what they are learning and how they move from surface, deep and transfer.
2. Expect students to consistently explain their thinking and justify their responses.

Feedback serves as a lamp that lights the path of those responsible for growth of the organization. Leaders understand the vision and goals of the organization. They know where employees are in relation to where they need to be. Through the eyes of vision, leaders provide specific feedback to help employees master their next steps and move into closer proximity to their individual and team goals. The leader fosters a culture of accountability by clearly and openly articulating the role of feedback in helping staff members reach their individual goals and in helping the school reach its goals.

Observation Cycle

Meaningful feedback creates an empowering force that leaves no person behind. It helps all staff members realize the need for refining their practice to help move the school towards the beckoning target they have identified. The phrase, 'feedback is a gift' has been adopted by the staff. Today, staff members embrace feedback and truly see it as a gift to them.

This section has primarily addressed feedback to improve student learning outcomes, however, vision does not limit feedback to one segment of the school population or for one specific purpose. Vision talks to the leader to instill the message that feedback is a universal condition for learning and an extremely important part of the continuous improvement process. It takes everyone working together to help the school achieve its mission and vision. Feedback builds strength by helping all members gain confidence and know that individually their role is vital; and they have a profound effect on the health and success of the school. When feedback is consistently provided to employees working in all areas of the organization it fosters everyone's understanding of their purpose and keeps the bar of high expectations clearly visible and easily within reach.

Appropriate training, feedback and dialogue with maintenance staff, cafeteria staff and paraprofessionals throughout the organization help them expand their knowledge and understanding of their role and they grow as professionals in each respective area. Today, the staff sees themselves as one team, pushing and pulling in the same direction to support their students. They realize that time is a factor and that winning could depend on their sense of urgency. The staff understands the relationship between feedback and their outcomes. They celebrate feedback as a gift knowing that where they are, is an okay place to be and just not an okay place to stay. When everyone comprehends the purpose of the organization and how they are connected to that purpose, vision grows from the heart of each individual, moves them to unity of vision and creates a beautiful image of what the organization can become.

Section Seven

Steadfastness

The Process of Vision

The series of steadfast actions taken over time define a process that creates change and leads to growth.

Vision enlightens the leader by revealing a clear and beckoning target that captures attention, creates internal excitement and draws contagious commitment. This empowering allegiance guides the leader's collaboration and methods of engagement to form a team that includes all of the stakeholders. The leader's clarity and excitement in communicating the vision are instrumental in the team's ability to see, understand and ultimately capture the vision. When the members of the team are armed with clarity, they are equipped to develop a comprehensive and continuous improvement plan with well-defined processes and strategies along with critical steps for implementation. The plan endorses the collective commitment to what the team sees. It identifies what the team values and how they will behave so that their collective efforts move them toward their vision.

When the vision is plain enough for members to recognize it from afar, in the mist of grim current realities, they are able to see that where they are headed is achievable and meaningful. The devotion to getting there provokes them to lay aside ineffective and unnecessary practices to spend quality time on what matters. Team members use their individual strengths and next steps as opportunities to empower their team. They understand that the best plan is ineffective when it is not implemented with fidelity across all segments of the organization.

Vision outlines the foundation of the process as one that members can honor by ensuring the following conditions are present: employees know the rationale for the work, expectations are clear and easy to follow, resources including training are readily available, employees have a voice in refinement and there is consistency.

Rationale: Staff members need to know the reason for the work. The clearness of each member to see where the organization is headed and understand the rationale builds and enlarges their vision and creates a buy in for the process.

Clear Expectations: Expectations that are clear and easy to follow erase doubt and uncertainty about what, how and when things should be done. They build organizational knowledge and empower the team to join their energy and increase team movement in the determined direction.

Resources: Everything employees need should be readily available to them. They should operate with the confidence that they can get what they need to do their jobs well. These resources include training individuals or teams need to increase their effectiveness.

Refinement: There should be a consistent method for regular evaluation of employees and employees should be engaged in evaluating the data from all segments of the organization. The culture listens to what the data tells it and is quick to release or refine any idea when it is clear that data does not support continuing.

Consistency: Members understand that the tools or activities are amended to help them work better and does not mean abandonment for the process. Vision keeps tools and procedures consistent. It allows time for members to know and understand the process and does not keep changing the rules. Consistency helps develop commonality and vision throughout the organization.

The process positions the school by helping it take root in the firmness of consistency, hold on to the familiar and develop strength of practice. It helps staff develop the right attitudes and inclinations to keep them steadfast on the journey. It is a frame of reference by which employees use as a basis for developing understandings and forming judgements.

Think about the foundation for your process. How is it similar or different from what is described here?	
Similar	Different
Reflections:	

Vision helps the leader make the process simple. It encircles the process and helps the team establish clarity by identifying specific expectations for staff members in all areas of responsibility. To help us define and clarify our process, we developed expectations throughout the school. We referred to these expectations as 'TIGHTS', because they were things that needed to be consistently implemented by all teachers. The staff valued meaningful work and understood that the expectations developed for teachers and support staff helped shape day to day practices, celebrations and contributed to positive culture within the school.

The charts below show school wide literacy and mathematics expectations (TIGHTS) developed by the staff as a part of the school's continuous improvement process. Teacher buy in was present and these TIGHTS were expected to be implemented in 100% of the K-5 classrooms. All teachers understood that these research-based strategies when consistently practiced would help our students learn at high levels. Strategies, instructional practices and processes are consistent across content areas and grade levels. This adds continuity for teachers and students.

School Wide Literacy TIGHTS	Grades	Start
Reading:		
Mainstream: 120 Minutes Daily	Structured English Immersion	
Curriculum: State Standards	Core/Supplemental Programs:	
Lesson Plans	K-5	Mon. A.M.
Components of Reading:		
Interactive Read Aloud; Shared Reading; Independent Reading; Accountable Reading	K-5	Day One
Differentiated Instruction: Guided/Small Group Reading	K-5	Day One
Fluency Practice; Daily/Fluency Homework Folder	1–5	
Supports:	K-1	Week 1
School wide Graphic Organizers		
Anchor Charts		
Literacy Notebooks		
Vocabulary:	K-5	Day One
Explicit Vocabulary Instruction	K-5	Day One
Early Literacy Learning:		
Phonemic Awareness, Phonics, Comprehension, Vocabulary, Fluency	K-2	Day One
Grammar:		
Grammar Wall, Concept Charts, Anchor Charts	K-5	Day One
Writing	K-5	Day One
Modeled Writing, Shared Writing, Guided Writing, Independent Writing	K-5	Week 1
Class Discussions: Students Express Thinking	K-5	Day One
Justify Response Using Information from Text /Source		Week 1
Agree/Disagree/Add on		Week 1
Differentiation: Small Groups	K-5	Week 1
Tier 2 Intervention	K-5	Week 1
Assessments:		
Daily Checks for Understanding	K-5	Week 1
Daily Ticket Out	K-5	Week 1
Weekly Common Formative Assessments	1–5	Week 1
Benchmark Assessments	K	Week 1
State Assessment	3–5	Spring
Progress Monitoring	K-5	Week 1

Mathematics TIGHTS	Grades	Start
Mainstream: 90 Minutes Balanced Math Block	K-5	Day One
Structured English Immersion:		
60 Minutes Balanced Math Block	K-5	Day One
Lesson Plans	K-5	Monday A.M.
Balanced Math	K-5	Day One
Math Review, Mental Math	K-5	
Story of the Day, Concept Building	K-5	
Graphic Organizer/Anchor Charts	K-5	
Math Check Point	K-5	
Differentiated Instruction	K-5	
Math Facts Practice	K-5	
Class Discussion: Students Express Thinking	K-5	Day One
Explain Thinking/Justify Responses	K-5	Week One
Agree/Disagree/Add on	K-5	Week One

Math Facts		
Kindergarten	+/– to 10	Week One
First Grade	+/– to 20	Week One
Second Grade	Master Addition/Subtraction Facts +/– to 20	Week One
January: Exposure to multiplication facts 0,5,10		
Third Grade	Review Addition, Subtraction Facts to Mastery Multiplication Facts to Mastery, Inverse Operation	First nine weeks: 0–8
Second nine weeks: 9–12		
Fourth Grade	Review All Addition, Subtraction, Multiplication Facts to Mastery, Inverse Operation	Day One
Fifth Grade	Review All Addition, Subtraction, Multiplication Facts to Mastery, Inverse Operation	Day One
Math Frames		
Kindergarten	Five and ten	Week One
First Grade	Ten and twenty	Week One

School wide system for solving word problems	K-5	Week One
Differentiation	K-5	Week Two
Tier Two Intervention	K-5	Week Three
Core Program:	K-5	Week One
Math Notebooks	K-5	Week One
Assessments:		Week Two
Math Screeners (F,W,S)	1–5	Week1–Week 2
Daily Checks for Understanding	K-5	Week One
Daily Ticket Out	K-5	Week One
Weekly Common Formative Assessments	K-5	Week Two
Benchmark Assessments	K-5	F/W/S

List your observations, thoughts, ideas opinions or remarks below:

What are some practices that are tight for both literacy and mathematics	
Literacy	**Mathematics**
What other content areas might these practices be appropriate?	
Explain how these consistent practices can be an advantage to building capacity within the school?	

A vision that is shared shapes the thinking that defines the organization. It helps the organization maintain focus and a healthy appreciation for the process as it moves through mountain top experiences. This same widely shared vision will build strength and momentum needed to steady the organization and push it forward during valley experiences. It will recall the clearly identified plan, evaluate the situation, identify next steps and maintain loyalty to the process. The process promotes steadfastness on the journey. Vision trusts the process through each phase of the journey. It helps the team refine as needed and stay with the plan through good and challenging times. The team's commitment to their plan will move them in the path of vision.

Throughout the process, the team identified antecedents of excellency, the qualities across the school population that contribute to their growth and development. They recognized that ongoing training, support and steadfast commitment to the process allowed them to use the learning framework by Douglas Reeves to identify their status as '**leading**'.

The Leadership for Learning Framework by Douglas Reeves	
Lucky	**Leading**
High results, low understanding pf antecedents. Replication of success unlikely.	High results, high understanding of antecedents. Replication of success likely.
Losing	**Learning**
Low results, low understanding of antecedents.	Low results, high understanding of antecedents. Replication of mistakes unlikely.
Reeves, D.B (2006) The Learning Leader How to Focus School Improvement for Better Results. *Alexandria, VA Association for Supervision and Curriculum Development. XX*	

The following are some of the important practices included in the process that allowed the organization to grow and develop.

Leading	
High results, high understanding of antecedents.	
The Process	**The Outcome**
Shared vision and collective commitments	'Yes we can' attitude was apparent
Clearly defined accountability system	The staff works in a spirit of synergy: Working together to achieve what they cannot do individually
Targeted professional development aligned with student learning needs	
Job embedded professional development process that supports implementation in each classroom	Culture supported immediate implementation and refinement of practice based on feedback
Regular assessment of student progress integrated into planning and instruction	Where I am is an okay place to be and just not an okay place to stay
Growth and progress are regularly celebrated	Celebrations are student and staff centered
Hard work and character are valued	
Effective grade level teams are recognized and supported	Staff work with a sense of vision, commitment and focus
Feedback is specific and authentic	Staff and students recognized feedback as a gift
Parent are valued partners	Parents attended regular parent classes, business, family fun and learning sessions

The process does not require instant recognition. Over time it creates an atmosphere where teachers and administrators understand and commit to the habits, practices and the foundations that allow students and adults to learn and thrive in an atmosphere of grace. It is just the way the school does business. Steadfast commitment to the process produced student learning results that placed our school among the leading schools in our district. Within the state, we were labeled as an 'A' School, a high performing school and high progress school.

Section Eight

Leader

The Character of Vision

The attitudes, features and distinctive qualities of noble character distinguishes the leader.

The character of vision is the secret sauce that holds up the pillar of leadership. You realize that the school is not about you; yet, it is everything about you. All traces of ego are habitually emptied out and there is the true power of constantly mastering yourself. Springing forth out of the root of humility is the fruit of openness, diversity and unity.

Vision plans, but it listens to counsel and weighs what it hears against the voice of reason and convictions. The leader has the disposition to accept that someone else's way may be better. The eyes of the leader see that within each person are limitless and untapped resources, skills and talents that make the organization rich with possibilities. The leader's mind moves beyond invisible lines and uses the winds of oneness to guide the organization through every level of development.

Vision informs the leader and the leader knows that one person can make a difference. You recognize your value, have the wisdom to recognize the value of others and understand that the greatest value is who you can become and what you can do together. You operate not as a respecter of persons, but as a person of equity, ensuring that every staff member gets what they need to confidently embrace their mission.

Vision perceives and grows within the heart of the leader and every member of the staff. It creates and sustains within their individual and collective domains, an atmosphere where each student feels safe and important. The staff members recognize that students have unmet needs and undiscovered talents. They are skilled at providing steady, constant, dependable and predicable support for students. Staff members understand that learning is a process guided by caring adults. They are competent in their ability to ensure that students develop strong cognitive and non-cognitive skills that are essential for success in school and in life. Vision focuses on the variables that are within its control by maximizing the hours within the school day. Together, they cross barriers, close gaps, work through challenges and connect with students.

Vision expects favorable results. Leading an organization requires the ability to guide it through peaceful and turbulent times. During times of calm, the leader perseveres in building up the organization through the continuous focus on training, support, feedback and data to identify strengths and next steps throughout the organization. The leader depends on assessment as an ongoing tool used to inform and direct services within the school. Vision uses data in all forms to give a clear factual picture of the current reality of the organization. It helps identify the areas of strength and celebrations as well as the most urgent needs within the organization. Vision within the leader works to celebrate the ways in which each employee perfects their craft and makes notable contribution to the goals of the organization. The high expectations of the leader inspire employees to work to transition their next steps to strengths. The leader has a well-developed and communicated process whereby next steps are refined and refinement is celebrated. This process includes the leader, but also functions independent of the leader. Celebration is a joyful, responsible and inclusive spirit that flows throughout the organization.

Vision assists the leader during turbulent seasons and helps navigate through the storms of conflict, confusion, resistance and disorder to steer the organization to its next level of calm. Vision recognizes that these unstable elements can rise rapidly and cause harm. The leader moves to eliminate the potential of harm by constantly mixing these behaviors with high expectations, purpose and data. The leader's commitment to the vision holds each individual accountable for operating within the established norms and in alignment with the purpose and goals of the organization. Clarity and accountability to these structures infiltrate the unproductive flow pattern, reverse the negative effect and direct the individuals to the solid foundation on which the organization stands. When employees know and understand their roles and how they will be held accountable, the organization forms inwardly one person, one attempt and one success at a time while shaping outwardly.

Vision is the DNA of success. The genetic information carried within the vision provides fundamental and distinctive characteristics that direct the leader. The complexity of visionary molecules contains all of the information necessary to help the leader avoid motionless movement by conducting business without purpose. They help the leader focus and move with intentionality. They guide the leader from one phase to another. These genes make the leader uniquely the leader.

The mental and moral qualities of vision help leaders send messages that allow them to build a foundation and connect on to their work; not erase and start over. The disconnect to vision is evident when leaders work to make immediate changes without considering the long-term direction of the organization. During a professional development session, the leader presented previous year's spring end of the year data that showed the school wide proficiency rate below 20% and as low as nine percent in some areas. The end of the first benchmark data was consistent with these results. As the principal facilitated the data session, teachers were asked to identify students who scored in the minimally proficient category they believed they could move to the partially proficient category by the end of the school year. This leader stated that growth and not proficiency was the goal.

Expectations that fail to define success as anything less than the academic proficiency and development of its students are unaware of the possibilities for success its DNA carries. Without the knowledge of its genetic make-up, the organization is in a constant whirl lacking substance to create forward movement. Attempting to lead without vision leaves one empty and disconnected to a sense of purpose. This emptiness and lack of direction should cause the leader to stop, use the experiential knowledge gained and anchor thoughts and actions deep into the fiber of vision.

The character of the leader governs the organization from a solid and moral foundation. It does not hide its honor; it exposes the light of high expectations and adopts strong practices.

Vision gives leaders the big picture that shows the desired end as it guides them through one step at a time. The leaders' understanding of the vision equips them to use words that cast a broad shadow and attach to the firm foundation of process. They see and communicate the goal while recognizing growth as simply a step in the process.

Vision is the voice of hope and victory that deposits desire within the mind and stirs up the 'I can' and 'we can' thinking. It monitors the mental and physical pulse and helps the leader tap into it in a way that forms a rock of thought and action that will inform and guide the leader into becoming bright pebbles of hope, direction and excitement. As these acquired stones are nurtured, the organization is layered with possibilities and achieves momentum that takes root and defies natural laws of doubt. These successes create immediate wins that sustain the organization through the forming, storming, norming and performing stages of development.

These four stages of development identified by Bruce Tuckman are used to identify the team's stages of growth.

Vision acts. It does not react. It shows the leader how to leverage key resources, capitalize on diversity and skills within the organization to create a culture that makes changes. Vision, the DNA of success, beckons and draws the leader to a desired aim that is larger than what has been voiced. The goal of vision is proficiency. In aiming for proficiency, vision understands that growth is a natural outcome and not the target. Vision put leaders in touch with their core values which embrace the belief that it is the right of every student to grow and move in the direction of proficiency. When proficiency is the target, it demands opening of the eyes of the mind which causes a shift in thinking and action that takes student learning from the back burner and places it at the forefront of the organization. Vision accepts no less. This process infuses the organization with oneness of purpose, attitude and goals and anchors it in vision. It helps the leader embrace new beginnings to set a new era in motion.

Summary

Vision knows the impact of healthy relationships within the workplace. It builds relationships as it works. It does not wait for relationships to form nor does it leap out in front of relationships. It begins by leading with respect and honor for all stakeholders. It engages others in a personable and inclusive manner that reveals transparency of expectations. It identifies the path that includes landmarks of success and watches strong vibrant relationships grow during the day-to-day work.

Vision is moving, its pace might change, its direction is known to shift, but it never stops drawing, guiding and calling. Through every phase, vision refines and looks for ways to improve. This fluid process of vision considers the phase and adjusts to advance towards the goal. Vision never finishes. It reveals more beautiful images of the picture it has imprinted in the minds and hearts. It keeps the team informed and steady in the process.

During hazy times, vision keeps the leader focused one decision at a time on the destination and the end results that resonates in the heart and lights the path. The navigation system of vision guides the leader forward. It has the power to illuminate the steps, prevent tragic reversals and keep the organization on the straight path toward effectiveness.